THE
TEAM
APPROACH

THE TEAM APPROACH

DARBY J. MINNICK, CLU, ChFC

The Team Approach
Changing the Way Financial Professionals Help Clients
Nonfiction

Text copyright 2019 by Darby Minnick

Any names, characters, places, events, incidents, similarities, or resemblance to actual persons, living or dead, events, or places is entirely coincidental.

Cover designed by Seedlings Online at www.seedlingsonline.com
E-book production by E-books Done Right at www.ebooksdoneright.com
Typesetting by Atthis Arts at www.atthisarts.com

All rights reserved. Except as permitted under the US Copyright Act of 1976, no part of this publication may be reproduced, stored in a retrieval system, or transmitted in any form or by any means electronic, mechanical, photocopying, recording, or otherwise, without written permission of the author. Every effort has been made to ensure that the content provided herein is accurate, up-to-date, and helpful to the reader at the time of this publishing. For information regarding permission, send a query to the author at info@darbyminnick.com.

Financial Representative, The Guardian Life Insurance Company of America, New York, NY.

Registered Representative of Park Avenue Securities LLC (PAS), 5 Centerpointe Drive, Suite 150, Lake Oswego, OR 97035, (503) 207-4550. Securities products and services are offered through PAS. Financial Representative, The Guardian Life Insurance Company of America, New York, NY (Guardian). PAS is an indirect wholly owned subsidiary of Guardian. Darby J. Minnick & Associates is not an affiliate or subsidiary of PAS or Guardian. PAS is a member FINRA, SIPC.

This material has not been endorsed by Guardian, its subsidiaries, agents, or employees. No representation or warranty, either express or implied, is provided in relation to the accuracy, completeness, or reliability of the information contained herein. In addition, the content does not necessarily represent the opinions of Guardian, its subsidiaries, agents, or employees.

Pinpoint #2019-83290 Exp 08/21

Visit www.darbyminnick.com for more information about the author, updates, or new books.

ISBN 9781689027939

CONTENTS

NOTE FROM THE AUTHOR

INTRODUCTION 1

THE MINDSET OF BUILDING A TEAM 7

THE TEAM STRUCTURE 19

THE FIRST STEP: GATHERING DATA 47

THE SECOND STEP: REVIEWING DATA 52

THE THIRD STEP: CHOOSING THE PLANNING PATH 54

THE FOURTH STEP: IMPLEMENTATION 59

CONCLUSION 61

BRING THE TEAM APPROACH TO YOUR WORLD 62

ACKNOWLEDGMENTS

ABOUT THE AUTHOR

This book is first dedicated to my daughter Natalie, who was convinced I needed to put on paper what I have been privileged to learn from other people in my career.

I want to thank all the people who taught me what I have tried to share here. I believe there are only a few times in your life where you get to work with a fantastic team, and I was allowed to participate in many fantastic teams over my life.

Lastly, I would like to thank my wife Cheryl. She allowed me to travel all over this great country to meet all these great people. Many a night, we said good night over a phone. Cheryl, I have been so blessed to have a person like you in my life.

NOTE FROM THE AUTHOR

This book will show you how business owners and high-net-worth individuals can benefit from a team of financial professionals.

We've crafted this book a certain way in order to meet the different needs of clients and financial professionals so that anyone can pick up this book and apply it to their circumstances.

Each chapter is written toward the financial professionals on a team (attorney, banker, CPA, etc.) and addresses how to make them more successful. However, we can't exclude the most important part of the team—and the reason the team exists—the client.

While not technically a "financial professional," the client is certainly integral and can benefit from reading this book and creating their own team and team structure. Because of this, we consider the client a critical team member for the purposes of this book.

No matter what role you play on the team, this book is written with you in mind, and all can benefit.

> *"What I love about team meetings is that I'm confident that when I die, my children will have met and worked with all my team members. The business succession plans will not be a surprise! This allows my business to succeed and be even stronger in the future."*
> *—Joe Billion, car dealership owner*

INTRODUCTION

After leaving college, I started selling in the auto industry. Not the most glamorous job, but it took me somewhere.

Ultimately, I became a leasing manager and eventually owned a third of a leasing company on the same property as a Chrysler dealership. Things were good—money was coming in for the first year.

That's when things went south.

My father-in-law and his partner were in the Chrysler business in 1978 when interest rates skyrocketed from 8% to 24% in less than two years. Chrysler was going bankrupt. During the second year, the dealership where I worked closed, and I had no income. I was married, had two children, and was going through a financial crisis of epic proportion. The other two owners in the leasing company went bankrupt, and I personally had to pay back all losses to the creditors.

Business is like that.

I had no way of knowing it would change everything.

That's when I pivoted to the financial services industry as a life insurance agent with Northwestern Mutual. I started to work in estate and business planning fairly rapidly. At the time, I had clients from my auto leasing business, my community, and a natural market of people who financed through me with Chrysler.

My brother was a CPA in the community where I lived. One

day, while discussing estate planning for life insurance to pay estate taxes, he said to me, "Darby, most of these guys who sell life insurance try to come in and show a big number that the client has to swallow in order to buy life insurance. If insurance salesmen would first figure out how to plan with the client like a CPA would, they'd have a more realistic number."

This started my thought process.

That day, my brother guided me to think about what I should be doing *with* and trying to learn *from* the clients. What I discovered was that the current approach wasn't working—I needed to do more than just sell insurance.

Together, my brother and I began to understand the advantage of working with an attorney and a CPA early in the financial planning process, not later. I started to see more realistic numbers, not something dreamt up that I couldn't back up with facts. As I employed this concept of working together, instead of independently, for our mutual clients, our team-oriented model began to draw other agents.

Six months into the life insurance business, I started joint work with other agents in the agency. Being from outside the life insurance industry gave me a different flavor for how to be effective, which helped my joint venture partnerships thrive.

My business and estate planning work grew. I would travel throughout Montana, working with other agents. Most of the time, I'd work with an agent and his best two or three prospects. Together we'd create a team and work through problems. I've been in countless discussions with other agents, CPAs, attorneys, business consultants, and more. This gives me a broad view of different circumstances that our clients face and how we can work together to form a sound plan and a safety net for the client.

I've seen it all.

Thanks to the power of this joint work with other agents, this concept of working together as a team expanded from a budding idea. Eventually, we grew it into a model that I've used to build a career forty years strong.

Now, it's time to take the team approach to the client's business.

> *"The idea that you have a team around you and your business is so important. The team concept saved me millions of dollars. When your advisors work with other business people in different walks of life, with similar challenges, we learn. Their life experiences with other clients helped my business because of the collective experience of all the people at the table."* —Ken Williams, mechanical and civil contractor

PART ONE:

THE TEAM STRUCTURE

"We're a third-generation, family-owned-and-operated business that my grandfather started nearly eighty years ago. My brother and I, along with a very dedicated and talented group of employees, work hard every day to deliver excellence to our customers. It's no secret that our longevity and success can be attributed to working with an exceptional professional team. The team pays close attention to every detail and understands the dynamics involved in running a family business. They help me come up with the best solution for any problem. I believe that the TEAM approach produces the best results because it melds people with different temperaments, talents, and convictions and leads to superior performance."
—Greg Beach, bus company owner

Chapter 1
THE MINDSET OF BUILDING A TEAM

Before we get into the details of building and working in the team (whether it's for your business or you're a financial professional working for a client), a discussion on *mindset* is imperative. Success in the team structure is all about the mindset of those on the team.

PMA Is Everything

Having a positive mental attitude (PMA) is critical to success. The majority of team members need to have a belief that they can survive any situation. They can achieve more than they think is possible . . . if they believe they can.

Cultivating a PMA by reading and listening to other people who have done what seemed impossible can help any team member understand that they can do the same. I have not only read and listened to learn new things, but I have watched clients and friends of mine do what no one believed was possible. When surrounded by people who stay positive through the most negative things, it's easier to believe it can work for anyone.

Having at least one or two people on the team who think like this (you can't always control who comes together) makes all the difference.

Don't Fear the Memo

When I moved to the next level in my estate planning career, I moved from Missoula to Bozeman and became a planning specialist for the General Agency. They had seventy agents at the time, so I traveled all over Montana to work with people in the insurance business.

One day, I traveled to Sidney, Montana. A team there was engaged in the process, and the sought-after insurance was already in underwriting. Then the client called and left a message. The other agent I was working with ran in and handed me a little pink memo that said, "The client wants to stop the process and not go through with it."

At this point, we had already worked with this client extensively. We had invested time and energy into this case. It was the biggest case the other agent had ever had in his career. After giving me the memo, the anxious agent asked me to call the client.

In my head, I thought, "He's terrified of what this memo could mean, so I have to deal with this problem."

Most people fear that memo because after sinking hours—even days—worth of time into a possible client, they could lose it all. The client would not only lose the insurance they need later, but the attorney and CPA would also never finish the work that will pay for their time. The client may never achieve the level of planning they require before they need it.

Thanks to years of experience with situations just like that, I've learned to accept and enjoy the memo. Having a positive mental attitude about a challenging situation has only bred more success for me. So, on this day, I wasn't afraid. I've learned not to fear the memo because there are plenty of wealthy people, and not enough time to serve them all.

Why wasn't I afraid?

Because you can't win them all. Calls like that happen on occasion . . . and that's OK.

Business isn't like the Super Bowl. Client prospects aren't one-and-done for the year. There'll be another client next week and the next week and the next week. The quicker a financial professional accepts that, gets rid of their fear, and moves forward with their team with a positive mental attitude, the quicker they'll see results.

How do they get rid of their fear?

Live in a positive mental attitude. Study books, hire a life coach, read through self-improvement books when you need a boost, and learn how others build a team with a positive mental attitude. If you build a team with PMA today, your team can live through any challenges in the future. You'll empower your team and clients to weather any difficulties.

Go Through the Fire

In 1980, we were broker than broke.

My small family was almost starving to death from the fallout of the car dealership closing, so we weren't in very good financial shape when I started the insurance business.

It seemed like every case that came my way had something weird happen. Or an unexpected challenge or issue would pop up. Nothing seemed straightforward or simple. I worried I'd starve to death if a case didn't go through or a client turned down an initial proposal. At the time, I didn't realize it, but eventually, these cases would supply some of my biggest growth.

Because, the hotter the fire, the greater the temper of your blade.

These odd cases and hairline sales forced me to battle my scarcity mindset. I had to believe that more clients would come—because what other option did I have? Instead of dwelling on the client who said *no*, I had to look for (or forward to) the one who would say *yes*.

The point is this—effective financial professionals look at the hard times as a sculpting period. They don't fight the fire—they go through it and come out the other side as something better. During those difficult days and strange cases, I lived with a positive mental attitude. I had to study ways to remain positive endlessly because it seemed like that was the only way out.

It was.

There's a picture by Charles M. Russell that hangs in my home now. The painting is of a hunter on the side of a huge mountain. The game he just shot is stuck on the side of a cliff about two thousand feet from the ground.

The name of the picture is *Meat's Not Meat Until It's In the Pan*.

Now, when I turn that picture over, on the back of it you'll see copies of the initial big checks I made in the insurance business. There's one check for $7,000 and one for $10,000. There had been a larger check for over $20,000 that I removed after the client decided not to put the plan in place (twenty days after the policy was delivered and paid for). The picture taught me the lesson that you can't win them all.

By the way, the client lost more than I did.

Meat's not meat until it's in the pan.

Keep It Moving

Oftentimes the client is uncertain about their situation.

There are many unknowns in business. Clients can be afraid to come forward or make needed decisions. This means they need to be pushed to keep the process moving.

It's the team that moves the client forward.

Sometimes the client gets stuck and can't move forward because of uncertainty or fear. If it was up to only them, they might not progress. The team *exists* to help in these situations—and the best teams make everything about the needs of the client, not about the needs of the team. This is where PMA and the collective experience of the team can be critical to help a client make appropriate decisions. The team helps them move forward to the next decision instead of staying where they're stuck or uncertain.

Let's take this to football.

Think of the team approach in parallel with the role of a defensive coordinator. They coordinate the strategy to protect the client and move the game forward. They all work to make sure that their respective pieces of the team are working together. They also help the client set up the appropriate legal structure and tax planning. Of course, sometimes the client can get too much momentum and start moving too fast.

The team comes along behind the client and makes sure they have all the i's dotted and t's crossed.

Check Your Egos at the Door

What doesn't look like a team?

One person attempting to control everything.

I've been involved with accountants, business planners, attorneys, and investment professionals who try to take over. That's not a team. They might be great, gifted, capable people who can provide needed help, but they've missed the point. The team collaborates to create the best possible outcome for the client and their family or their business.

Everybody currently playing on a professional football team will be gone in a number of years, but the team will still exist. The same applies to businesses.

For example, let's say I make a proposal that my client should buy a significant life insurance policy. Across the table is the client's CPA, attorney, banker, and perhaps a business consultant. If I'm a true team player, the plan I present to all of them focuses on the needs of the client—not my commission—and the other team players chime in.

The CPA figures out that the client can afford it and that it would fit the situation. The attorney may help with the legal concepts and asset protection, while the banker suggests what role he can play. The client hears the other financial professionals—which builds trust—because all their recommendations are focused on the client.

In other words, the work with the client is not about the

financial professional. If a financial professional can't deal with that, they get off the team.

Anybody can die and never again have to deal with their business or their family situation. But the people that really buy into the team concept realize that a group of people is there to help them and their family get through anything. The common goal for the team isn't one and done. They're creating something that will outlast all of the team members, including the person they're working for. All financial professionals are going to quit, retire, or die. But these particular businesses and families will live on.

After forty years, I've realized that the beauty of having the right people on the team is that the client or family will still have the best possible outcome given what they're contending with. No matter what happens.

That is teamwork.

> "I can't think of any better business decision in thirty years that has better helped grow myself spiritually, mentally, and physically." — Don Kaltschmidt, owner of a car dealership

Darby Doesn't Dance

I don't chase anybody.

To clarify, I don't call clients or team members I don't have a direct relationship or interaction with. If I'm being brought into a deal to advise, I try to have someone more central to the deal call the interested parties and bring me in on the phone or to lunch or whatever the case may be.

Not only does it strengthen the team process when someone else does the introduction, but it provides safety for the client.

And when a deal doesn't go through? That's fine. I move on. I don't dance around the lost opportunity because there are too many people needing my help and not enough time to dance with an agreement that wouldn't benefit everyone.

Don't dance with those who don't want to work with the team. Move on. Too many other people need help.

Businesses Are Families

The best businesses are more than just the work they provide. Some of the businesses I work with have employed people for decades. That changes things when one thinks about what would happen to the business if the owner died.

In the end, the best businesses are just like families. What I've found through the years is that the team can be part of that family.

A good team involves not only just the business owner, but their family members as well. It's common for me to be in regular team meetings with the children and spouses of my clients. There's more at work than just business here.

For that reason, the team helps the client deal with issues that come up on a business *and* on a personal level. Working on a team requires changing a previous, transaction-only mindset. Instead of seeing the client as a one-and-done deal, pivot until the team becomes a sort of family.

This shift will help engage the entire team for the good of the client. Ultimately, having a business family with engaged, motivated people focused on the health of the family is good for everyone.

The Cost of the Team

Believe it or not, cost is a mindset issue, and it can affect the team.

I'll use a clothing analogy. The guy that first taught me how to dress properly at a haberdashery taught me that *quality* creates value. Some clothes cost more money, but I'm paying for the quality of the piece to last. If I didn't pay, the clothing wouldn't have the long-lasting quality I wanted.

The quality is not the price.

The focus shouldn't be on the price paid, but the value received. Working as a team to create the best outcome for the client isn't about the price the client pays. It's about the value they receive. The price is about what is *gained*, not what it costs upfront. It's not about what the client does because of the team, but the poor decisions that they *don't* make because of counsel of the team.

No matter how this works out, the client has to pay for the team meetings. Yes, they can get expensive. But, the team can help them understand how the benefits multiply down the road, whether in security for their family or business, or in growth. It helps if the team supports each other so that the client understands that the bills from the other financial professionals are worth every penny.

For example, one of my clients had a business take off. He wanted to buy something that cost an incredible sum of money but, on the counsel of the team, decided not to. Then an economic downturn hit right after he would have purchased it. That downturn could have dramatically affected him in a negative way had he gone through with the purchase against the advice of the team.

The cost of the team that year helped him save millions.

All team members support the client's needs by supporting each other. It's a mindset to support each team member instead of just supporting individual interests. This develops trust in the whole team because the other financial professionals are affirming that something is important, not just the person that would earn the sale.

Let's pretend I propose that a client buy a policy that costs $40,000 of premium per year for a need in their world. The client is aghast because they've never thought about spending that much money. Naturally, they'll look at me and think, *He's just out for the commission.* If the other financial professionals say, "You know, I think that fits your need even though the premium is quite high compared to what you've paid before," that will help dissipate the pain based on the price. The policy is a solution to the client's situation. When another team member can affirm the necessity of the policy, that builds trust with the client. The team doesn't protect each other's sales, commissions, or fees, but are reflective and speak up for the good of the client.

This takes pressure off the client. They won't think they're buying a policy because somebody wants to make money.

> *"The team is absolutely worth the investment of pulling them together. The amount of money that I saved by taking their collective advice and avoiding investing in a bad business is hundreds of thousands of dollars. When I think about the amount of value that I receive in that short amount of time, it's better money spent paying my financial professionals together than meeting with each person for an hour individually. It takes more time to solve it meeting individually than together."* —Mark Easton, owner of a construction business

It's a River, Not a Pond

Change the mindset that the work stops at a transaction.

In a team, the work will always continue. I like to say that the work with the client flows like a river. As part of that, the work never ends. Team members review the plan regularly with and for the client.

Regular life insurance agents will finish a deal, and then the client doesn't hear from him again unless there's potentially another sale. If the agent even called back and tried to sell them something, most people would be shocked to hear from them.

Whether you're an attorney, CPA, life insurance agent, or investment professional, business is often a transaction. It's a transaction to do an estate plan. It's a transaction to do a business succession plan. It's transaction when the team meets and pieces that stuff together. They come in and solve the problem, and they're done.

With a team, they do what I just described, but then *they review it the next year*. The plan is a river, not a pond. It never stops. It continues on forever. When a client gets a team that commits to reviewing policies again each year or when an issue arises, that helps prevent mistakes and continues to create the best value for the client.

Tax laws change, business planning shifts, economic conditions move, people age, family members die. What happens to a business when there's a divorce? It's a horrific event that affects the family, but it also impacts all the employees and people connected to the business. The team is there to help the client, business, and family flow through the process.

If the insurance industry stopped being salespeople and started being financial professionals at this level, we could change the world for a lot of clients.

Chapter 2

THE TEAM STRUCTURE

Now that switching to a team mindset and cultivating a positive mental attitude is on your mind, let's lay out exactly what a team looks like.

> *"In the team model for a successful practice—for any practice, really—you need key people that can help you implement and follow through. The team model is perfect because there are technical experts that the team can refer to the client. In my job, it equates to 100% more success."* —Bryan Davis, Guardian Life Insurance Company, Senior Consultant, Business Resource Center.

Generalists vs. Specialists

Before we dive into the specific financial professionals on the teams that I've worked with over the years, let's define broader terms. Members of the team often come down to two types of professionals: generalists and specialists.

Generalists, if working with the client, usually have the client's trust. Generalists need to know 100,000 things. Most importantly, they need to know when it is critical to bring in a specialist, and be willing to let that happen. Ego shouldn't stop them from getting the right help. Most accountants and attorneys are generalists. They often have to be—their fields are wide.

Specialists, such as a tax attorney, know a lot about one specific field. They help advise the team around specialty questions. The team may need a specific specialist at certain times, but not all the time.

There's a give and take between the generalists and specialists in order to support the team as a whole. The specialist needs to be cognizant of working with the generalist (who has the trust of the client and a longer relationship in general), and the generalist needs to be willing to give way for the specialist's knowledge.

If a client doesn't have a specialist, and one is needed, team members should provide trustworthy recommendations. Word-of-mouth is the most typical engine.

Many major life insurance companies have specialists in their home office that work in business and estate planning. These specialists typically don't work with the client—they work with the financial professionals. If a financial professional needs to find a reliable specialist for their client, they can call the general agency in the client's area and ask for recommendations local to the client.

Which is one more reason it's so critical to have a strong team.

Bryan Davis is a gentleman I've often brought in as a specialist from a home office. In a number of cases, he's helped team members by providing research from the tax world that shows how the IRS may feel about our planning. He has exposure to many people all over the U.S. (as well as the special planning they're doing). When he provides all that extra information in these planning stages, it helps the team do the best planning possible.

Success in the team relates directly to knowing what each financial professional does and how they can serve the client.

Next, we're going to discuss each team member, their role, and how they can improve their current performance to make the strongest team for the client.

1. Certified Public Accountant (CPA)

As a general rule, the most trusted person on a team is typically the CPA because they know all about the client's finances.

Most people would rather talk about their miracle romance with their wife than let somebody know the specifics of their income tax bill. But the CPA, by virtue of being the CPA, has to know their financial statements.

Before the team even forms, many clients already have a CPA or consider their CPA part of their team. They should be respected within the team on the merit of their understanding of the client's situation alone.

— Role in the Team

The CPA is here to reflect to the client what the client needs to see—they can initiate ideas and support the client through providing a financial picture.

Some of them go above and beyond doing taxes (which tends to be the case for the most successful CPAs), but others are mostly interested in the numbers. The CPA should be supportive and helpful for the client and the team in whatever capacity they are wanted or needed.

Many business owners consider their CPA as just a

recordkeeper or historian. The team model asks more of the CPA. We need a proactive-thinking planner. If the current CPA doesn't want to be proactive with planning, that's fine. But they need to be willing to allow someone into the team who will be, such as a specialist accountant who does specific planning work.

The specialist isn't meant to step on the toes of the existing CPA who files the tax returns, of course. We want to respect their role in the team. But we bring in a specialist for analysis on some of the special accounting for a temporary period of time.

— Fee Sensitivity with CPAs

> *"I was thinking about buying a big ranch. We didn't structure it well upfront. I didn't know I'd structured it wrong, and eventually brought it up at a team meeting. They helped me restructure in case my partner and I split up and have likely saved me a million dollars in taxes."* —Clint Lohman, serial entrepreneur

Let's talk a little bit more about CPAs that are used solely as a recordkeeper instead of something more.

An issue I've seen throughout all my team experience is that clients are often fee sensitive. Because of that, they fear running up a big bill. By doing so, they underutilize their CPA. More than once, when we've started to engage with the client and show them plans or possibilities, they've asked, "Why didn't my CPA tell me this before now?"

I'll say, "Let me ask you—when's the last time you sat down with your CPA and asked, 'What's the fee you charge for income tax or estate planning above and beyond doing taxes?'

Or when's the last time you said, 'Why don't we run a tab for ten hours and start figuring out different ideas for income tax planning and estate planning?'"

Once I ask that, the client looks at me like, "What?"

That's the point.

The client may not have asked their CPA those questions because they're fee sensitive (or perhaps they didn't know they could ask) and were worried about running up a bill. This goes back to the power of the team backing up the roles of the other financial professionals.

For the CPAs who find themselves in this situation and want to know how to manage it, or further build trust with the client, here's how to do it.

My big brother Lynn (who first brought the team idea to my mind and has been doing this for fifty years), told me how he works with his fee-sensitive clients.

> *"When I'm done doing the tax return, and they've signed it and have the bill already, I say to the client, 'If you have fifteen more minutes, I'd like to talk to you about an idea not on your billable time. I'd like to spend fifteen minutes with you talking about an overview of estate planning at no charge.'"*

He's already explained that they don't have to worry about getting a bill and that he's giving them a concept that they may or may not choose to use. This approach clears the air. Some say, "No, I don't have any interest."

That's OK. Nothing ventured, nothing gained. Sometimes they say, "OK, let's schedule something."

Then you have a chance to start building further out.

— The CPA as a Team Member

This is what a team-oriented CPA looks like:

- **Willing to learn more.** Imagine that the team comes up with ideas that have ramifications for the client's estate tax or income tax. If the CPA were to say, "I've never heard of this strategy or plan before, but let me study it and get back to you," that's a team-oriented CPA.
- **Speaks for the team.** While working with a client on a complex idea, and during a meeting in which I didn't attend, a tax attorney said about one of my ideas, "You can't do that. It's wrong." The CPA didn't agree or disagree but said, "Wait a minute. Let's call Darby and give him twenty-four hours to address your issue and see if he has a response for what you're thinking. It could be 100% correct, but let's give him twenty-four hours." She calls me and explains the situation. In twenty-four hours, I have a response. Turned out, the attorney hadn't understood everything I presented. Once I explained further, he said, "Oh, I see now that it'll work." Thanks to the CPA speaking on behalf of the team, we negotiated better outcomes for the client.
- **Proactive.** When we showed a CPA how to use our planning software, she asked for a meeting with our mutual clients. Then she sat down in a room with all of us and said, "This planning software is going to cost $10,000 in fees for our firm to load your information into it, because it's very complex. But what I think we'll gain is cutting

down our timeframe each year going forward for us to complete your financial statement. You'll pay less each year because of this tool." A proactive CPA sets out the financial terms of an investment like that.

Of course, not every CPA will want to be involved at a deep level, and that's fine. If a CPA isn't very actively engaged in the team, we certainly don't alienate that person. We're going to need them every year to be involved in tax returns. Any of the additional things we'll need when tax law changes will also drive us back to the CPA, so it's important to help them feel like they're part of the team inasmuch as they want to be.

2. Attorney

In a team, the attorney isn't just any attorney.

To be really effective in this kind of team, an attorney needs knowledge of tax law, including business and estate tax planning. With attorneys, I see a lot of generalists and specialists because clients come to us with whatever attorney they began with. Many attorneys become close to people and can be influential in the family.

If the client's attorney is open to working in conjunction with a specialist, that's the best of both worlds. The client will still have their day-to-day operations with their trusted attorney, and the team will still have occasional involvement with them. But the tax attorney can help bring in the needed specialty experience.

Quite often, the following happens when I start talking

about an attorney with a client. They'll often say, "I already have an attorney."

"What do they do?" I'll ask.

"Oh, I think he helped write up our will a while back."

"So, he must be a business and tax attorney, right?"

They normally appear quite puzzled and ask, "No, what's that?"

That's when I explain that a tax attorney is somebody who understands the law but also understand taxes, which opens the door for us to start moving the client in that direction.

— Role in the Team

When we're talking about a team player who is a tax attorney, it's not the guy who does real estate transactions. It's not the person who sues people, and it's not the person who provides counsel about marriages and wills.

We want attorneys who are good at counseling with a broad knowledge of tax, business, and estate tax planning.

— The Attorney as a Team Member

A really good tax attorney can take a very complex tax planning idea and make it easy to understand. They can draft a great legal document that may become fairly deep and complex. Having the attorney do a summary letter or a picture of the plan has been a big asset in getting the team on the same page—and helping everyone understand the big picture. Attorneys who have been comfortable if the client desires to record or videotape his explanation of the plan have also been helpful to our clients.

> *"We spend lots of time in our business going to meetings around the country to improve our techniques and profits. Those improvements are valuable . . . but they're pennies on the floor compared to the millions of dollars we can save in estate taxes, and income taxes, with proper business planning! Proper business succession planning can save millions for your children, not thousands!"* —Joe Billion, car dealership owner

3. Life Insurance Professional

If you ask a hundred people (especially age thirty-five and younger) what their experience has been with life insurance agents, expect ten of them to say, "I've had a good relationship with a life insurance agent."

We think that's a better-than-average estimation.

Why?

Because most people don't even interact with life insurance agents anymore! They either don't get a chance, or if they do, a buddy who isn't even in the business anymore sold them life insurance.

With a team approach, we crystallize an ideal life insurance agent into someone who's mostly concerned with the greater good of the client and being there for them when needed. Their own income is secondary.

That's not what most expect from the life insurance profession.

While speaking with a client from Hawaii about their business planning, we found out that someone from our larger organization could work with him in his own area. We offered to have someone local be his life insurance professional because we knew it would be better for him to have someone where he was. We'd lose any potential sales—but that didn't matter.

I said, "Here's the deal. Let's see if a local agent works out for you, because it'd be good for *you* to work with someone in Hawaii."

He paused and said, "You know Darby . . . that's what I like about you. You're more concerned about the greater good than yourself."

He went to a local financial professional in Hawaii.

— Role in the Team

The primary role of the life insurance agent is to identify catastrophic threats that exist now or may exist in the future. They should anticipate threats and ways to efficiently insure against them, or create a contingency plan if the insurance can't be obtained.

For example, in personal planning, the life insurance agent should ask the question, *What if the breadwinner dies? Can we insure for that risk?* Yes. And we should. In complex planning, we can plan for transferring a business to someone else. Take the classic problem when a child, who is critical to the success of the business, dies during the business transfer plan.

Without a backup plan, that's a problem.

With one life insurance professional in particular, I remember being excited when they brought a presentation to the whole team. They let the team review their suggestions for the life insurance policy, instead of just the client. I loved that.

One time I mentioned to one of our clients that we might be able to use life insurance in his planning. He said, "Well, maybe it's time to start thinking about that."

The next time we had a team meeting, I brought it up to the team and let the team think about it in conjunction with the client. That's not me selling him a policy—that's me bringing it to the team.

When you think about how to operate within a team environment, look for the team members to love the idea presented, hate it, or give input. People really good at this won't let the negative input affect them. They'll know that it's advice from the other team players that may be pertinent for this particular client.

— The Life Insurance Professional as a Team Member

A team-oriented life insurance professional may look like this:

- Do things that support client trust.
- Present the proposal to the whole team for analysis.
- Avoid becoming aggressive or defensive.
- Be willing to do what's best for the client and not themselves—even if they lose out on commissions.

The best way I can describe a team-oriented life insurance professional experience is through a story.

Somebody brought us a client with very complicated planning needs. The client had lots of life insurance with a good life insurance company, but he disliked his life insurance agent. He had a huge amount of insurance he needed to convert from term to permanent within a very short period of time. The case would end up paying a $50,000 commission.

He asked me, "Why don't you become the agent of record instead of him? Take it. I don't like the other guy."

"The other guy has to do it," I said. "He's the one who did the work to get you to this point, and if I take over and do it, it's going to look like I did it to get the money. If the agent hadn't done what he did, you wouldn't have the chance to convert it, and you couldn't buy it today."

I called up the other insurance agent, started working with him, acquired all the ledgers, and clarified what was going to happen. The other insurance agent waited for me to tell him how much he had to pay me or for me to cheat him out of the deal. It's been four years now.

He's still waiting.

That's not who we are. And now who's a member on that team? We are! We have the client's trust because we did the right thing. That's what happens when people know the financial professional is on *their* side.

What I've found, after all this time, is that people hate to be sold. But they love to go shopping with friends.

4. Investment Professional

A lot of people tend to ask, *Why is it important for these entrepreneurs to have an investment professional on the team?*

Let me follow up that question with a question: Do you have a car with a spare tire? How often do you use it?

Most people have maybe used their spare tire once. On my current vehicles, we've never used the spare tire, and it's not that we don't *have* flat tires. We just haven't used the spare yet.

THE TEAM STRUCTURE

Now, let's say you're thirty miles into the country, in the middle of nowhere, in a blizzard, and your tire goes flat. There's no cell service. Boy, are you glad you have that spare, I bet! Most people think they'll never use it. When it's needed, however, it's critical that they have it.

It's the same with an investment professional.

Many of our clients are business owners and entrepreneurs. One of our clients, many years ago, met with his investment professional right after selling a two-million-dollar business venture. At that time, he had a lot of cash. He was hoping to invest the money and get a great rate of return. The investment professional told him the best that could be done was to beat inflation over the long run. He told our client the best thing to do was to reinvest the money with his own skill in business. He was right.

The client recently sold his latest business venture for tens of millions of dollars. Many business owners see investing money in the same way.

They know that:

1. They get the best return on their money by investing in their own business where they have talent and control.
2. They have enough risk already in business that it doesn't make sense to invest anywhere else that requires risk.

A good investment professional loves to analyze risk vs. reward in financial markets. It's their focus. They're someone who understands the needs of the client and that part of the client's capital that will be invested in the market. We like to use that knowledge to help the client. Then, one day, when the client sells a business, or the family has a liquidity event, there is a trusted financial professional already on the team to manage and invest the money wisely.

— Role in the Team

When it comes to advising on investments, the team should have someone who has built a knowledge of and relationship with investment opportunities. If someone passes away and millions of dollars of life insurance benefits land on the family, the investment professional is on the team to help them navigate that.

For example, a client may be selling their business for fifty million dollars and will need to reinvest the money wisely. Or consider the small business owner whose primary investment is their business—their wealth can be destroyed rapidly. Having all that risk can present opportunities for wealth disruption, and we want to mitigate that risk.

One client and his brother each own half of a profitable company. They have a buy-sell agreement funded with life insurance. If either one of them passes away, their business interests are going to be liquidated and automatically paid for in cash. Millions of dollars will go to the spouse and the children. They will need to have experience and exposure to a professional that the family trusts and believes in, because they're going to get a tremendous amount of money.

In the team paradigm, the investment professional can show the client how to diversify and split their assets into different risk categories. The team can take a perspective on this to help the client feel more comfortable when they proceed.

An investment professional is out there trying to make

returns like an offensive coordinator would for a football team. (To play this out, we consider the insurance guys to be the defensive coordinator.) We're trying to make sure that, no matter what happens, the client always has some capital.

— The Investment Professional as a Team Member

- A team-oriented investment professional will give their opinion on investments and opportunities and how they fit into the client's future.
- They really understand the client's needs and that those needs should be taken into account when investing the client's capital.
- They help with the decisions around how a client should allocate money among different assets, such as real estate, private businesses, or the stock market.
- They help analyze the risk of different investment opportunities.
- They help the client understand how their investments are or aren't correlated.
- If the market takes off, and the client wants to move his money there, a good investment professional will call a meeting to redefine objectives before taking action.
- They won't receive the investment money without a team meeting.
- They have a functional knowledge of many investments in the stock market.

One particular client we worked with was really excited about gold. During a team meeting, the investment professional gave a presentation and went over the last 150 years of history of gold. The how, what, objectives, and more. He *clarified* and *educated*. He didn't take a stand, but informed. Not only did the client enjoy being informed, but I loved it because I could apply it to other people I worked with.

When you have a great investment professional like that, everything they say is interesting, on point, and truthful.

5. Banker

> *"Most financial professionals feel more comfortable in the team setting, where they feel like they are a member of something bigger. It acknowledges their value, sets a respect level prior to arrival, and generally gives a level of decorum that promotes people working together well." —Tom Swenson, Bank of Montana*

Some people may not consider their banker a member of their team, but bankers can be a crucial safety net.

They bring their shared experience to the table when most small business owners don't have a CFO. A banker becomes a quasi-CFO for the business. Think of it this way: bankers don't lend money to repossess assets; they lend money to get money back.

Banks are parachutes, and they're elevators. The idea is that, in tough times, having the right bank on the team slows the decline of the business. In good times, leverage can accelerate growth.

When things are really going well, a bank can take them higher. When something goes wrong, and their business world contracts, without the bank's cash, the business could be crushed. We've seen people who didn't have a banker on their team get into very difficult situations.

— Role in the Team

Great bankers, the ones we enjoy working with the most, will tell a client that if they receive a better deal from another bank, to go sign the paperwork. They help the thought process around collaboration.

For example, one of our clients has significant real estate holdings where they operate their business. Like many clients, their real estate is held in a separate entity from their operating company. They were thinking about refinancing the whole package, which included significant loans from several financial institutions with great long-term rates. They were the first and second lien holders on the property, and it was going to be a complex transaction.

Another bank made a proposal—leave all the existing financing in place, and this new bank would simply be the third lien holder. The banker on the team didn't hesitate to tell the client to take that deal as fast as possible.

A team-oriented banker works for the client. With them, I sit back and watch them try to figure out how they can enhance the client's world. Most bankers have to figure out what is in their shareholders' best interests. It's their job to protect the shareholders' money as much as they can. But a team-oriented banker is one step beyond that. They're worried about the client *and* their shareholders.

The banker is also going to be able to give more perspective on private investment opportunities. Ask them the question,

"If you were going to lend money to acquire this business, how would you look at it? If you were going to lend money to do XYZ real estate project, what feedback would you give?" Then they can give their perspective as the lender. Bankers know how auditors think, and that's helpful on a team.

Again, it goes back to what's best for the client and not for the individual.

— The Banker as a Team Member

- On the team, the banker is the person everyone looks to for debt and cash-flow questions.
- The banker can step in like a chief financial officer.
- They deal with all the finances.
- Many people are afraid that if they tell the bank everything, they won't lend them all the money they need. That's not always true. Banks chase small businesses because they're often good businesspeople.
- The client may first need to accept the thought process of bringing in a banker, whether that banker lends them the money or not.

6. Business Consultant

The classy saying is that a business consultant comes in, charges an entrepreneur money, tells them what to do, and leaves.

The big four accounting firms in the country have huge entities comprised of business consultants. Let's say the client has done a magnificent job with their business, but they still may not know the best practices for everything. The business consultant can come into the team and help the client increase productivity, net worth, and salability.

If a client thinks it will take ten years to build their business, the business consultant can help them see how to enhance their assets and cut that time down. When a business owner properly plans to exit their business, they should be spending less time in their business, not more. A business consultant can help the client see how the business can operate more without the founder in a way that gives the business more value, or makes it more dependent on the key people and less dependent on the founder.

One business consultant we have enjoyed working with is Len Hornung. He specializes in deeper business planning. He has his internal team use software to calculate his clients' budgets and cash flow. They give an overview of where the business is and how to take it to another level to optimize the clients' objectives.

— Role in the Team

If a client wants to retire, a good business consultant will help them figure out how to get the most out of their business when they're ready to sell. They figure out how to build as much value as they can while building the business, and how to extract that capital someday. A good business consultant will help a client understand where they're at, where they're going, and how to get there.

A business consultant can also help a client transition from a founder mentality to a CEO manager mentality. For example, the generation after the founders of the business has to be better at running the business through the financial statements than the founder, because the business is usually bigger.

When someone—specifically the founder—leaves a business, a lot of the major employees and key people end up leaving as well. One family I worked with for years ended up in a transition phase when the father wanted to retire. I knew Len Hornung and his associate could come in, consult with the family, and help them figure the transition out.

We had Len come in, study the situation, conduct a meeting with the key players, figure out how to adjust it differently than how the father ran it, and provide some tools. Len called a big meeting with all of the key people in that organization and said, "Here are the options. One: You could sell the entire company to somebody else. Two: We can transition this company to the son and his team over the next few years. Three: We find a CEO to run the company for the next five years, then transition to the son."

They voted on what they thought would be best. In the end, the team didn't have confidence in the son to take over the business. Now the client had to worry about who they should bring in as the CEO . . . but, of course, the team knew of a firm that could send a person in to help.

Sure, the business was transferring from father to son, and the team worked on it together, but as the father transitioned, so did the team. The business consultant helped that happen much more smoothly.

— The Business Consultant as a Team Member

- Help the client get the most out of their business when they're ready to sell.
- Help the client stay focused on the business.
- Help the client increase net worth and salability.
- Help the client understand where they are today, where they're going, and how to get there.

7. The Client

Let's go back to football for a moment and reflect again on the fact that there are teams with no single owner. One team is owned by a community corporation—basically the residents of the city. That's why there's no owner's box. On the other side, other football teams have a team of people that work for the owner to help the business run.

Just like football, the client creates the team. The client is the most essential part! There is no team without the client.

One thing the client does that no one else does is become empowered through having the team. They bring vision, creativity, opportunities, and problems to the team. Thanks to the team, the client receives advice, makes informed decisions, and leaves more confident than before.

There's a natural growth for clients as they foster a team environment. I've seen it many times. The client pulls together their team, takes ownership of it, grows it, brings up issues for counsel, and becomes a better client.

Sometimes their vision for the business is foggy. Sometimes they need glasses. And as strange as it sounds, sometimes financial professionals have to relate to the client how successful they've become because the client hasn't noticed.

For example, somebody might bring me into work with a client who's worth twenty million. They're still busy trying to build a business and make it run properly. When I ask them, "When you started out, did you inherit a lot of money?" they might say, "No, no. I didn't have any money. My wife and I started with ten bucks and a suitcase."

My response is always the same. "The really tough part for today is you still don't know that you're wealthy. I'm here to tell you that you're so wealthy the government expects half of what you've earned when you die. You went from broke, to wealthy, to the government's going to take half that wealth."

We'll get clients who work hard for five to ten years, then realize that their net worth went way north. They just didn't even think about it because they're so busy running the business!

The client also brings vision, problems, and ideas to the team so they don't have to do it alone. A team-oriented client is empowered by a good team, and the team becomes empowered by having a good client.

— Role in the Team

While clients vary, I've seen similar types over the years. Some clients want to build a bunch of wealth and then do something else. Others want to build an organization or structure, even

THE TEAM STRUCTURE

with their family. An empire builder wants to create something that goes beyond them and their world. Those are typically great clients.

Sometimes the client makes a big decision, then has a team meeting and tells them what they did. Other clients will engage the team in the decision-making process first—which is the best use of the team. That's where the client takes advantage of the multiplier effect. The team can speak into a dilemma to create better results. They're giving their thoughts before the client acts. Then the client makes their own decision.

We had a really great client who wasn't looking for everybody to say *yes* to his ideas. He didn't even mind if the people on the team occasionally dissented. He listened to both opinions and often encouraged the team to present differing opinions to help clarify their own thoughts. Then he made his judgment.

— Client as a Team Member

- They have vision.
- They view money as secondary. It doesn't matter to them that they're worth fifty million dollars because it's about what they're creating for the people around them. The more they give away, the more they receive.
- A really great client isn't looking for their team to agree with them about everything at all times. They often seek many opinions and points of view about a decision they are trying to make. Once they have the perspective of everyone on the team, they make their decision.

> "Knowing that I went through the process of making a very informed decision is the biggest thing about the team structure. I'm not doing this with just one other person's input. I have four to five people's input, from all their different expertise. They all have their strengths. Because I've worked with them for a while, I know their strengths and their weaknesses. I can think about what they say to me and formulate a better-informed decision." —Don Kaltschmidt, owner of a car dealership

8. Technology

While not technically a team member, technology can be a fantastic asset, and it's worth mentioning. One day, I received a call from a client who said, "My father's probably going to die in the next day or two. We have a lot of concerns."

We immediately set to work and pulled up everything pertinent we had on that client. We dealt with this surprising and difficult situation for the family. The attorney got back to the client within a short period of time. Another six hours later, we were able to instantly communicate with the family about their concerns because we had everything we needed at our fingertips.

Thanks to shared technology, we could help them.

— Role in the Team

Having an operating system that all team players have access to, and that has all the information about a client and their world, is a huge asset to the team.

It needs to have the capacity to take different scenarios and show what could (or will) happen under certain circumstances. For example, a family member may pass away. What would happen with estate taxes for the family? With the right technology, the team can find out. If I get an email from one of my clients about something they want done, I can pull up all their prior records and financial data to figure out how to make that work for them.

The program should show cash flow, financial assets, business planning scenarios, taxation, and more.

PART TWO:

THE TEAM PROCESS

"I, like many people in my position, had not focused on my own planning. I had no estate plan, taxation planning, life insurance, or written, enforceable living-and-upon-death will. Now I have all of those things in place, and it simply wouldn't have happened without the team discovering these basic needs. More than 20% of my business activity is as a result of team meetings. I currently have more business opportunities than I could hope to pursue, and that is a direct result of creating my team."
—*Tom Swenson, Bank of Montana*

Chapter 3

THE FIRST STEP: GATHERING DATA

The team process is built to connect everyone in the team so they can plan contingencies and act quickly when the unexpected occurs.

For example, when one of my clients goes to the Mayo Clinic and does an executive physical, they go for five days and participate in many tests. Their medical team then provides a list of current conditions and future risks. The client doesn't have to take care of those things all at once. They can choose what actions to take that day and plan to address other parts of the assessment in three years.

The team process works in much the same way.

Contributing members use software to aggregate client data and provide a snapshot assessment of the client's current financial situation. They can then communicate with the client about what the client wants to do with their assets and discuss possible futures. The team utilizes their individual skillsets to draft legal documents, generate an estate plan, and create contingency plans for the unexpected.

Let's look at how the team process begins. The first step is gathering data.

Gathering Data

When I was first exposed to the insurance industry, I heard that

I needed to get the *feelings* of the people and the *facts* of the people. That approach continues today.

The team process starts with gathering two groups of information: hard data and soft data. This holistic approach yields an incredibly detailed picture of where the client is, where they've been, and where they'd like to go.

Gathering hard data is straightforward—just gather all financial data and documents. All that data goes into the database or software that the entire team has access to. This process starts when the financial professional offers a questionnaire to the client in order to catch the hard data. That's followed by the delivery of supporting documents. Every data point on the questionnaire should have documentation to go with it.

For example, if the client gives a number for how much money is in investments, they need to supply account statements to back that number up. If they put down that they have a car insurance policy, the financial professionals should get documentation on that policy.

Why so much emphasis on documentation? What the client believes they have is not always what they really have.

I sat down with a client for a data-gathering meeting and asked for general information about his world. During the course of the conversation, I asked how much he and his spouse had in savings.

He said, "Well, we've got $20,000, maybe $30,000 at the bank."

"Great," I said. "Get your last statement from the bank, and send it over to me."

A day later, he calls me up to let me know that they had over

$350,000 saved. He said, "You know, you try to save a nickel, and you throw it in a bank, and you forget it. And I guess I had forgotten that we've been doing that for a long time. It surprised me how much we had in the bank!"

That's why hard data is so important.

Soft data isn't much harder to gather—it just takes a little finesse. Soft data refers to the client's goals and concerns. Now, a financial professional can be very sterile in their approach to gathering soft data. We're not talking about that scenario. That approach isn't going to allow the team to really understand anything about the client.

I'm talking about *getting to know* the client.

If golf enters into the conversation, don't fight it. Talk about golf for a few minutes. Eventually, the financial professional can swing the conversation so they can get a better idea of the client's fears and dreams. That doesn't come from filling out a piece of paper. By the time the conversation is done, the financial professional should know where the client wants to be in three years and ten years. The financial professional should ascertain the client's feelings, understand their situation, and determine how what they want relates to what they've got.

There's homework to do with the soft data. A client once sent me information about himself, but I decided to go to their company website and read through it from there because all businesses with websites post their stories for the public. That website story is a great example of how what the client perceives about their business may be different than what they show to others.

When it comes to gathering facts (hard data) and the feelings (soft data), a lot of times both will come out as the client talks about their objectives. The conversation about objectives benefits from using a timeline to frame the client's thinking.

For instance, at three years, they'll be thinking about short-term goals and concerns. Then ten years enters the conversation, and suddenly those goals become a little more robust and complex. Finally, planning is brought up about end-of-life and the future of the business beyond the life of the client.

Some questions that will arise include questions about which family members are to be included in the planning. Will the kids be taking over the business? What risks or concerns need to be raised for the different time periods? Are there key employees to consider?

I can't stress enough the importance of this holistic approach to data gathering.

A financial professional needs to know everything *to the best of their ability* about the client and their situation. Unfortunately, this is not always the case for some financial professionals.

Take my industry, for instance. Some in the life insurance profession try to get clients to give them only as much soft and hard data as they need to target a transaction. They may ask, "How can I sell this person this product right now?" instead of "How can I understand what this person needs now and in the future?"

While some life insurance agents push a client to get a physical so they can sell a policy, the team simply needs to know the client's health and life expectancy.

The financial professional should be thorough enough to find out if the client is even insurable, and getting a physical is critical to discovering that fact. It's also information the client needs in order to have an informed discussion with the team. If a physician tells a client he's got a 30% chance of living five years and a 10% chance of living ten, the client might want to know that when planning for their future!

Talking with a client about the facts and their feelings opens and closes doors with regards to their available options. With the data laid out, financial professionals can try to understand the client's situation.

Chapter 4

THE SECOND STEP: REVIEWING DATA

The client doesn't always know whether their data is complete or not. The team can help them know if it is.

Once the financial professional feels they've gathered both kinds of data to the best of their ability, the team moves into the second step of the process: reviewing the data.

The financial professional doing the bulk of data gathering should have somebody on the team verify its completeness and accuracy. This might require a meeting with the entire team to confirm that the findings are correct and accurate.

In *Star Trek*, the original series, the characters play chess on three levels for the same game. The game had seven different boards and was called *tri-dimensional chess*. When the team is reviewing data in preparation for income tax planning, estate planning, or business with family, it's like getting ready to do tri-dimensional planning.

Like having three levels of chess, the team needs to review data thoroughly.

As an example, let's say there are two clients: a husband and wife. The team of financial professionals think they know the clients' situation and which individual owns each asset. Then one of the clients gets a potential terminal disease and could pass away in six to eighteen months.

The team goes into action and starts looking at the balance sheet. (This is where the tri-dimensional chess game starts for

THE SECOND STEP: REVIEWING DATA

the team.) In most states, assets need to be allocated twelve months prior to an end-of-life event. Most clients have no idea about this, which means that they might not have accounted for it in the data gathering phase. The team needs to be sure that the right assets are in the right person's name so that it flows through the estate properly. The team shouldn't be doing an initial review of the data at this time because there just isn't time. They barely have enough time to adjust the clients' planning to accommodate the end-of-life timeline.

When a real event happens, the team will need to dig to the very bottom of the data and ensure everything is in order. The trick is, if the team does their initial review as soon as the information is acquired, *and* the client understands the need for complete data from the beginning, any reaction to a real event will lead to planning that's responsive and accurate. The team and the client win.

That's playing tri-dimensional chess.

Chapter 5

THE THIRD STEP: CHOOSING THE PLANNING PATH

The third step is the planning path, which is where the team determines the client's current financial position.

Based on the data, what type of planning should the team pursue in order to enhance the client's actions and yield the desired outcome? Is the team really in the business of maximizing profitability? Retaining key employees? Securing the stability of the family, should the client suddenly pass away?

These goals can be allocated to three planning phases: the value-building phase, the business-exit-planning phase, and the estate-planning phase.

The Value-Building Phase

One of the initial questions we ask people is how they started. One time, a client said, "Well, my dad had a small business, and he asked me to come join him at some point to work with it. Within a year or two, he decided he wanted to retire. But then they changed the laws of how the business worked, and we expanded greatly."

Now, that didn't tell me the whole story. What I learned later was that, when the father decided to retire, he walked into the shop, handed my client the keys, and said, "I'm done." Then he walked out and never came back.

My client had to figure everything out from the ground up by himself—down to finding the locks each key went to. While he was going through this difficult time, the state government changed the laws governing his industry. One thing my client had managed to do during this time was to maintain all of his father's connections to institutions that were tangential to his business. Due to this, he *was* able to expand greatly.

At the same time, however, he knew the law could change back. During that period, he worried about losing all of his business, which was making all of the money for his family and employees. He started to invest in other businesses, to diversify his cash flow, and to become a serial entrepreneur. He went from one core business and diversified into other businesses to try to have other streams of income that would not all disappear at the same time.

This was his value-building phase, which the client had moved through before he came to me.

The Business-Exit-Planning Phase

"The important thing that I've learned while doing exit planning is that when we want to move a client successfully through the transition to get their business to the person of their choosing, at the right time and at the right price, you need to have team players. You have to have them all playing in the same sandbox together. Everybody knows what everybody else is doing. We become the facilitators and then bring in the experts to facilitate the plan. We help the process and make sure that we give clients fall-back positions."
—Len Hornung, Certified Exit Planner (CExP) and Financial Advisor of Park Avenue Securities

When a client is in the business-exit phase, they face a particularly stressful pitfall that can sometimes arrest their forward movement: moving from one income level to another.

Where before they had $50,000 of discretionary income, they could be coming to this next phase with something more like $500,000. The pitfall is that there is a danger of their lifestyle changing to account for the $500,000. That's a lifestyle they could get used to real quick.

The serial entrepreneur client from the value-building phase example knew that. He played conservatively with his lifestyle, then diversified his investments.

Another client of mine sold their business, and two of their key employees decided to leave the business at that time. These two employees then convinced one of my other clients to help them start the same business in a different part of the state. They created the business, and he provided the capital. The two employees turned it into a great business, and they built value for themselves and my client over time.

The client above, along with his two key employees, knew the importance of diversification as well. When the business matured, it became very profitable. It went through the normal downturns that every business does, but the client still sold it for a considerable sum.

Now, let's talk about key employees.

Often, in the business-exit-planning phase, my clients want to do something for their key employees because they see them as the greatest asset to the business. Most businesses have a financial statement that shows the liquid assets, long-term assets, liabilities short and long, and equity. Key employees of the business are one of its greatest assets, yet they're not on a financial statement.

When we start working with people and talking to them about growing value or exiting the business, we make it clear that when people buy businesses, they buy the total global picture, including the financial statement and the key employees. The employees, in many cases, matter but are not included in the ask when purchasing the business.

This serial entrepreneur had long-term employees that had been with him forever. Eventually, he sold that business. Two months before the closing of the sale, he called a team meeting. He said he had a couple of key people, and he wanted to discuss what he could do for them. Even though he was selling the business, and they'd be gone, he wanted to do something for their long-term employment. He wanted private plans for them that would pay a half a million dollars or three-quarters of a million dollars when they retired. His desire didn't have anything to do with the purchase agreement and wasn't part of their employment.

He did it because he cared for them.

That's a team player.

Estate-Planning Phase

The estate-planning phase involves planning for what the client will need for the rest of their and their spouse's lifetime—and then what to do with the surplus above that.

Sometimes the surplus goes to the kids outright; sometimes it becomes a trust that will take care of the family for many generations to come. Sometimes it goes to create a foundation, or sometimes it supports a charity. The point is for the wealth to go where the client wants it so that as little wealth as possible is destroyed by taxes.

One time, when I was a part of a team selling a business to a major corporation in a tax-free exchange, I sat people down with the client and his spouse while the sale was still pending and said, "The next year of your life will be the most difficult year of your life financially."

The spouse looked at me like I was crazy.

I continued, "You've got more cash than you've ever seen at one time in your life because of the sale of this business."

"Well, what do you mean?"

"When's the last time you had five million in your checking account? That's why it's going to be so hard."

Often, lottery winners don't know how to handle their winnings. Those same people will say that winning the lottery was the biggest burden they ever had in their life. People are unaccustomed to a lot of capital and don't know what to do with it. Sometimes it's devastating to themselves and their families.

The team can prevent that.

Too much wealth is one of those little things that most people don't have any concept of because they've never had it happen. They've never had a lot of capital show up at one time, whether they earned it or it came through somebody's death. If they've got a great team that can help the family or the survivors deal with the shock of death or the burden of a lot of capital at one time, they have a good safety net.

That's the importance of a team.

Chapter 6

THE FOURTH STEP: IMPLEMENTATION

> *"It took about two or three years to get my team off the ground because my business planning was kind of a mess. I was busy just making money. I was so used to doing things with nobody except for a CPA that I had no real structure to anything. I just went kind of crazy and started a bunch of businesses. Getting the team together helped me bring all the professional people around me and get my head wrapped around the organization and a plan. It helped me plan where we were heading—instead of going where it takes me."*
> —Clint Lohman, serial entrepreneur

Once a train is on the tracks, it still needs people working the engine. It needs fuel. It needs tracks that are still in good working order. It's great to have train tracks, but without maintenance and with the wear-and-tear of life, tracks don't mean much.

The same applies to the team structure.

It's great to do all this planning and have meetings, but if the team doesn't have any documents signed, it doesn't mean much.

For the team, implementation means helping everybody understand where the tracks go from here until the end of this person's business experience or life. At this stage, the team has gathered and reviewed the data and defined the client's planning path. They've laid out the plan and engaged as a team to take action on each of the financial professional's areas of expertise.

The team needs to service the train on those tracks continually.

The client's plan needs to be maintained on a continual basis. The financial professionals need to be abreast of what the client is trying to do, and what they are doing, with the other team members.

This team orientation isn't a quick fix. This is a long-term, constant service. I've done the proper planning all the way through for a client and assembled a great team. When the client passes, the team comes together. All the businesses are liquidated to the partners of the client's business in a pre-specified method. Money goes to the surviving spouse, and both the investment professional and insurance professional make sure the surviving spouse receives what they're due and helps them plan how to use it for the rest of their life.

That's how it should work.

The implementation phase will often take a lot of time to complete. Timing and workload will vary from client to client, but normally, this step will take six months to two years to get all parts of the plan implemented. This might seem like a lot of time to some, but keep in mind, each team member and the client have businesses to run apart from being on the team.

For most people, the hardest part to clarify is how long it's going to take to run this plan. The team has accomplished the initial phase, built the tracks, linked up the train, obtained the coal for the engine, and built the railroad tracks. The train has left the station.

Now, how long is the team going to run it for?

For the life of the business or the client.

CONCLUSION

You don't have to create a team for your clients, or even for yourself. There's certainly no requirement for it in the marketplace, and you won't see other financial professionals doing this as a rule.

But why wouldn't you want to?

In the course of all my years in insurance, I've seen businesses and people come and go. But it's the team structure that helps those businesses remain . . . and continue to change the lives of all the people they touch.

Build your positive mental attitude. Find other financial professionals you can trust. Begin to implement the team structure one piece at a time, and you'll start to change your own life, as well as the lives of your clients.

That's the team promise.

If you're interested in working as a financial professional on a team, or want to build your own supportive team, we can help. Keep reading for more information.

BRING THE TEAM APPROACH TO YOUR WORLD

with Mike Hixson

I've worked with my father-in-law Darby for thirteen years. In that time, I've seen the team structure completely change the lives of the business owner, the lives of their families, and the lives of their key employees. It's come down to two major changes:

1. The team has accelerated the growth of our client's business.
2. The team stops the client from moving forward with bad business deals.

Working with Darby has given me a unique perspective on how to make this a successful process for each client, and it's a process we work hard at every day. It wasn't long before we realized that we needed to encourage clients to engage all their financial professionals at the same time and build their team. That's why we created this book and have additional resources for you to get started now.

If you are a financial professional and want to bring a higher level of service to your clients, we can help you out. Or, if you're a client that wants to pull your team together, we can help with that too.

Go to www.darbyminnick.com/resources for exclusive access to a sample agenda for your first team meeting, implementation guide, and more.

ACKNOWLEDGMENTS

Thanks to Joe Billion, Clint Lohman, Don Kaltschmidt, Greg Beach, Bryan Davis, Len Hornung, Mark Easton, Tom Swenson, and Ken Williams for being part of this book and an integral part of our team.

ABOUT THE AUTHOR

Darby Minnick's passion is to make a positive difference in other people's lives. He works on behalf of clients around the country with the help of his business partner and son-in-law, Michael Hixson. Darby lives in Montana with his wife and enjoys spending time with his children and grandchildren. Find out more about the Team Approach at www.darbyminnick.com/resources.